The Think Book . . . .

The Think Book . . . .

The think book of quotations

To help you figure your way out when it seems there are none . . .

Bishop Leviticus Fordham Sr.

Library of Congress Control Number: 2011961149
ISBN: Hardcover 978-1-4653-0759-0
Softcover 978-1-4653-0758-3
Ebook 978-1-4653-0760-6

This book was printed in the United States of America.

CONTACT INFORMATION:

bishop1234lf@yahoo.com
And:
Leviticus Fordham on Facebook

To order additional copies of this book, contact:
Xlibris Corporation
1-888-795-4274
www.Xlibris.com
Orders@Xlibris.com
108418

CONTENTS

THE THINK BOOK

OF

QUOTATIONS

HERE AND NOW

OF

A SON, HUSBAND, FATHER AND PASTOR

This book is dedicated to my wife Diane, our four children Caprina, Leviticus jr, Joshua and, Sondra, also my grandchildren. For they all helped me in this book, in putting it together and making sure I never gave up, and also to make sure I seen this book all the way to the end. Each one of you has made a profound impression on my life.

For many years my mother and father would quote so many things; some that seem to not make any sense. When I began to get older it all started to make complete sense, and over time it kept me inspired and guided me through many of my own experiences. Over time I began to quote myself. And this is how this book came to life, from the quotes of my parents and quotes of my own. This book is made to make you think as the quotes did with me.

This book has been designed to make people think before they reacted, and if they have already done so to help them figure out how to get out of their situation, also to not get to many people involved when you can work the situation out on your own. We all come to a point in life when we must learn to work things out in the right way, and to help them consider carefully to whom to seek advice when needed.

Anger is an emotion related to one's psychological interpretation of having been offended, wronged or denied and a tendency to undo that by retaliation

CHAPTER 1

ANGER

1. ANGER IS THE ONE THING THAT COMES IN OUR LIVES AND BRINGS MANY REGRETS LATER.

2. ANGER SO MANY TIMES WITH ACTIONS BRINGS DESTRUCTION.

3. ANGER HAS CAUSED DIVISION AMONG FAMILY, FRIENDS, COWORKERS BROKEN RELATIONSHIPS CAUSED THE DEATH OF MANY. AS SMALL A WORD AS IT MAY BE. IT HAS MANY DESTRUCTIVE WAYS WHEN IT COME SO MANY TIMES WE DON'T THINK JUST REACT WHEN IT IS FINISH DEATH HURT AND DESTRUCTION IS STARING US RIGHT IN THE FACE. IT IS ALRIGHT TO GET ANGRY BUT IT IS NOT ALRIGHT TO USE ANGER AND DESTROY OUR SELVES AND OTHERS ANGER WILL COME BUT WHEN IT DOES HANDLE WITH CARE.

4. AN ANGRY PERSON WITH PLENTY OF MOUTH SHOULD AVOID ALCOHOL.

5. IT IS AMAZING HOW WE CAN BE ANGRY WITH SOMEONE AND AS SOON AS WE COME IN CONTACT WITH THEM THE ANGER CEASE.

6. DONT TRY TO MAKE SOUND DECISIONS FULL OF ANGER IT COULD LEAVE LASTING PAIN.

7. SO MANY TIMES WE HOLD ANGER BECAUSE OF PAIN WE HAVE FELT BECAUSE OF SOMEONE OR SOMETHING AND BECOME FRUSTRATED WITH EVERYTHING AND EVERYONE BECAUSE OF IT

8. DONT LET ANGER TURN YOU INTO A BEAST OF NO TRUST AND NO FAITH IN OTHERS MISTAKES HAPPENS.

9. PAIN IS IN THIS LIFE DON'T LET ANGER INCREASE THE PAIN. FORGIVENESS REALEASES ALL KIND OF ANGER.

10. NO MATTER WHO WE ARE WE WILL GET ANGRY SOONER OR LATER BUT WE MUST LEARN TO CHANNEL THAT ANGER TO GOOD.

11. YOU CAN USE THE ANGER OF AND ENEMY TO BRING YOU VICTORY.

12. ANGER CAN BUILD A WALL BETWEEN TWO OR MORE CEASE FROM ANGER AND THE WALL CAN COME DOWN.

13. ANGER IS FOUND IN EVERY HOUSE BUT ONLY LOVE CAN HOLD IT TOGETHER.

14. ANGER CAN ONLY LIVE A SHORT WHILE WHEN UNDERSTANDING COME IN.

15. WE SHOULD GUARD AGAINST THE THINGS THAT CAUSES ANGER.

16. AND ANGRY PERSON CAN BRING EMBARRASEMENT TO THEMSELVES AND OTHERS.

17. THERE ARE TIMES ANGRY SPEECH CAN BRING RELEIF.

18. ANGER CAN HAVE A CLEANING EFFECT.

19. ANGER CAN CAUSE A SHARP RESPONSE.

20. PICKING A FIGHT WITH THE WRONG PERSON BECAUSE YOU ARE ANGRY CAN CAUSE YOU A LOT OF PAIN.

21. ANGER USED PROPERLY CAN COME WITH BENEFITS.

22. ANGER CAN LEAD TO A LONG AND PAINFUL DEFEAT.

23. IT IS AMAZING HOW WE CAN GET ANGRY WITH OTHERS WHO MAY NEED OUR HELP WHILE THINGS ARE WELL WITH US AND WHEN THE TABLE TURNS WE WANT THEM TO TREAT US WITH CALM.

24. WE SHOULD LEARN TO CALM DOWN JUST AS QUICKLY AS WE GET ANGRY.

25. A PERSON THAT IS A PEST CAN BRING ON ANGER.

26. WE CAN GET ANGRY WITH SOMEONE ELSE FOR SOMETHING WE DID.

27. GOOD IS ALWAYS THERE BUT MANY TIMES IT HARD TO SEE THROUGH THE EYES OF ANGER.

28. NEVER HASTE TO BE ANGRY.

29. A WISE PERSON KEEPS THERE COOL EVEN WHEN THEY ARE HEATED IN ANGER.

30. A CALM MAN THINKS MUCH CLEARER THAN AND ANGRY MAN.

31. DON'T ALLOW ANGER TO REST UPON YOU FOR TOO LONG.

32. DON'T LET ANGER CAUSE YOU TO ACT IN THE WRONG WAY

33. LEARN TO LOVE MORE AND TO GET ANGRY LESS DO WHAT EVER IT TAKES TO STAY AWAY FROM ANGER.

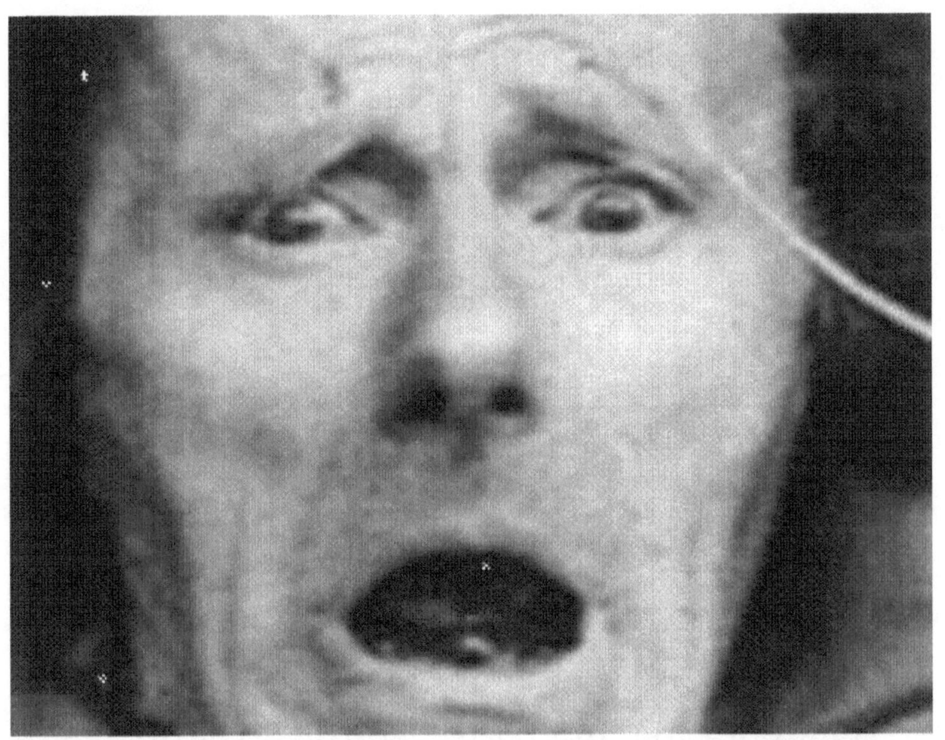

FEAR: a distressing emotion aroused by impending danger, evil, pain, etc., whether the threat is real or imagined; the feeling or condition of being afraid.

CHAPTER 2

FEAR

1. FEAR IS A THIEF IT CAUSES YOU TO MISS OUT ON THINGS THAT HAS BEEN PREPAIRED FOR YOU.

2. IF WE CAN ONLY GET PAST OUR FEARS THERE IS NO LIMIT AS TO WHAT WE CAN ACCOMPLISH IN OUR LIFE.

3. TO FEAR GOD IS THE ONLY WISE THING TO DO. TO FEAR ANYTHING ELSE IS TO BE IN PRISONED.

4. FEAR FIND FAULT, THINK FINISH BUT NEVER DOES,IT BRING FAILURE AND DEFEAT IT HIDES IN A CORNER, IT RUNS FROM THE FIGHT OF LIFE, AFRAID TO MAKE DECISIONS FEAR IS ONE OF THE WORST ENEMY THERE IS.

5. DON'T LET OTHERS DOPE YOU INTO A BAD DECISION BECAUSE OF FEAR.

6. DON'T BE OVER COME WITH FEAR BUT OVER COME FEAR WITH COURAGE.

7. MEDITATION, PRAYER AND FAITH CAN HELP TO OVER COME ALL FEARS.

8. FEAR ONLY ALLOWS US TO SEE THE SITUATIONS AND DOWN SIDES NOT THE FINISH PRODUCT OF FAITH.

9. FEAR BRING SO MUCH UNREST WHEN WE LEARN TO PUT FEAR AWAY FROM US WE FIND PEACEFUL SLEEP.

10. FEAR KEEPS TAKING FAITH KEEPS GIVING.

11. FEAR SHOULD NEVER BECOME A FRIEND OF YOURS IT WILL STUNT YOUR GROWTH.

12. IF YOU FEED YOURSELF FEAR YOU WILL RECEIVE IT IF YOU FEED YOURSELF COURAGE YOU WILL RECEIVE IT.

13. FEAR BRINGS DIVISION THAT ONLY TRUE FAITH AND UNDERSTANDING CAN PUT BACK TOGETHER.

14. FEAR AND DOUBT CAN PROLONG EVERYTHIG IN LIFE.

15. BEING AROUND COWARDS ONLY INCREASE FEAR.

16. WHEN YOU ALLOW FEAR TO COME IN THE ONLY PERSON THAT WILL GET RIPPED OFF IS YOU.

17. DONT ALLOW FEAR TO DO YOU AS THE TONGUE IT CAUSES SO MUCH TROUBLE AND WHEN IT IS FINISH IT HIDE BEHIND THE TOOTH.

18. LIFE IS OUR GREAT TEACHER BUT IF YOU ALLOW FEAR TO TEACH YOU YOU WILL ONLY BE A DROP OUT.

19. COWARDS LIVE IN FEAR AND COMES BY THE THOUSANDS. COURAGE COMES BY THE DOZENS.FEAR WILL MAKE YOU A COWARD AND STAND BEHIND EVERYONE AND EVERYTHING.COURAGE STAND UP FRONT AND HIDES BEHIND NOTHING OR NO ONE. TO BE A COWARD AND FEARFUL IS THE EASY WAY OUT OF ANYTHING BUT TO BE CORAGEOUS IS NOT ALWAYS THE EASY ROAD TO TRAVEL.

20. BEING FEARFUL NOT ONLY BRING PROBLEMS FOR YOU BUT ALSO FOR OTHERS AROUND YOU. IT HOLDS UP YOUR LIFE AND THERES.

21. FEAR CREATES THINGS THAT ARE NOT THERE WHEN YOU TURN THE LIGHT OFF FEAR ARISE AND WHEN YOU TURN THE LIGHT BACK ON EVERYTHING IS STILL THE SAME AS WHEN YOU TURNED OUT THE LIGHT.

22. FEAR WILL NOT ALLOW US TO STEP OUT ON FAITH BECAUSE OF PAST FAILURES BUT ONCE WE LEARN THAT

FAILURE IS WHAT MAKE US SUCCESSFUL THEN WE WITH PATIENCE TAKE IT IN STRIDE.

23. THERE ARE SO MANY OF US WHO SAY WE DONT LIKE PAIN. WITH ALL THE PAIN THAT FEAR BRINGS APPARENTLY WE DO.

24. FEAR KEEPS US FROM THINKING ABOUT THE POWER THAT IS WITHIN US TO CHANGE THINGS.

25. FEAR KEEPS YOU FROM GOING THROUGH THINGS OF PURPOSE TO KEEP YOU FROM THE WAY OF UNDERSTANDING AND CRIPPLE YOU IN EVERYTHING.

26. SQUEEZE OUT FEAR AND ENJOY THE RICHES THAT THE LORD HAVE LAID UP FOR YOU.

2Co 5:7 for we walk by *faith*, not by sight

Mar 11:22 And Jesus answering saith unto them, Have *faith* in God.

CHAPTER 3

FAITH

1. HOLD ON TO FAITH IN THE TIME OF TROUBLE IT WILL LEAD YOU OUT ALL OF LIFE DARK PLACES.

2. JUST BECAUSE YOU STEPPED OUT ON FAITH IT DOESN'T MEAN THAT YOU WILL GET IMMEDIATE RESULTS ALL THE TIME. SOMETHINGS YOU HAVE TO HOLD TO THE FAITH AND KEEP GOING.

3. HAVING FAITH DOESN'T GUARANTEE YOU EASY TIMES THERE ARE TIMES GIVING UP COMES TO MIND SO MANY TIME WHEN CONTINUES PRESSURE IS PLACED UPON YOU. IT SEEMS THE BEST WAY TO GO BUT IT IS'NT. FAITH WORKS PATIENCE WORKS HOLD ONTO YOUR FAITH.

4. ONCE YOU HAVE BEEN SHOWN THE DIRECTION IN WHICH TO GO POINT YOUR FEET IN THAT DIRECTION AND GO. WALK IN FAITH LET IT BE YOUR EYES OF LIFE.

5. SO MANY TIMES WE SPEAK OUR VISION PREMATURELY AND BECAUSE OF DELAY MANY WILL MOCK. NOT KNOWING THAT YOUR WALKING IN CONTINUOUS FAITH WILL BRING IT TO PASS.

6. AS LONG AS I HOLD TO MY FAITH NO ONE OR NOTHING CAN BREAK ME OR CAUSE ME TO LOSE MY FOCUS NO MATTER HOW GREAT THE PRESSUE.

7. WHAT I BELIEVE THAT I WILL ACHIEVE NO MATTER HOW LONG IT MAY TAKE MY FAITH WILL BRING ME THROUGH.

8. I SEEK TO ONLY MAKE GOOD CHOICES EVEN THOUGH I MAY HAVE MADE SOME BAD WHICH LEAD ME TO A PATH OF HEART ACHE AND PAIN BUT THROUGH MY FAITH GOD HAVE ALLOW ALL THING TO COME TO MY GOOD.

9. WHEN YOU ARE READY TO DO SOMETHING WHAT KEEPS YOU FROM DOING IT NOT SURE, DOUBT, NERVOUS ONCE

THE SPIRIT SPEAK TO YOU GO IN FAITH AND THE END RESULTS WILL MAKE IT SELF.

10. WHEN YOU WALK OUT IN FAITH SOMETIME THINGS MAY HAPPEN QUICKLY SOMETIMES DAYS TURNS INTO WEEKS. WEEKS INTO MONTHS INTO YEARS BUT THE WHOLE KEY IS HOLD TO YOUR FAITH.

11. A FAITHFUL PERSON IS A BLESSED PERSON EVEN THOUGH YOU MAY GO THROUGH SOME DRY SPELLS YOUR FAITHFULNESS WILL BRING DOWN THE RAIN.

12. INTIMIDATION DOESN'T WORK ON THOSE OF FAITH.

13. THE HEART OF A FAITHFUL MAN WILL BRING FORTH ABUNDANCE HIS STRENGTH CAN CONQUER ANYTHING HE FEEDS HIMSELF ON GOODNESS AND RECEIVE PROSPERITY AND SUCCESS.

14. A PERSON OF FAITH KNOW THAT THIS WAY IS NOT A SPRINT BUT A JOURNEY A PATHWAY OF CHANGE A DESTINY WITH VICTORY AT THE END.

15. BUILDING SOMETHING COMES WITH A LOT OF SWEAT. LET DOWN DISCOURAGEMENT, DISAPPOINTMENT, AND PEOPLE WALKING AWAY FROM YOU. EVEN FAMILY TURNING AGAINST YOU AND FINALLY YOURSELF BEING DISCOURAGED BUT THE ONLY THING THAT KEEPS YOU GOING IS THE FACT THAT YOU ARE A PERSON OF FAITH NOT EVERYONE IS.

16. WITH MY EYES I CAN SEE FAR WITH MY FAITH I CAN SEE FURTHER.

17. A PERSON OF FAITH DO NOT NEED TO CONTINUE IN THE COMPANY OF THOSE THAT ARE NOT OF FAITH THEY WILL ONLY HELP TO STEAR YOU IN THE WRONG DIRECTION.

18. WHILE WALKING IN FAITH YOU MY INCOUNTER THINGS THAT APPEARS TO BE FAILURES DON'T BE FOOLED BY THE ILLUSION THINGS OF THIS NATURE ARE A SIGN OF BEING ON THE RIGHT PATH.

19. FAITH IS HERE TO TAKE THE NOTHINGNESS OUT OF OUR LIFE.

20. FAITH WILL LEAD US INTO ALL FULFILMENT.

21. FAITH PREPARES YOU FOR THE THINGS TO COME.AND DURING THE PROCESS OF TIME YOUR FAITH WILL BE TRIED. THINGS MAY BE TAKEN AWAY YOU MAY LOSE THINGS FAILURE AFTER FAILURE. EVERYONE LOOK AT YOU AS BEING A FAILURE. YOU START THINKING DIFFERENTLY AND FEELING DIFFERENT BUT WHAT EVER YOU DO DON'T LET GO OF YOUR FAITH AND JUST HOLD ON UNTIL THE WIND BLOWS OVER AND THEN YOU WILL SEE THE LIGHT.

22. FAITH WILL CAUSE YOU TO NOT LOOK AT WHAT YOU ARE GOING THROUGH BUT WHERE YOU ARE HEADED TO.

23. WHILE WALKING IF FAITH SO MANY TIMES THINGS IN OUR LIFE WILL NOT GO RIGHT BUT WE MUST PRESS ON.

24. OUR FAITH HELPS US TO OVER COME FEAR AND DOUBT IT TEACHES US ONLY TO BELIEVE NO MATER WHAT JUST BELIEVE.

25. FAITH ALLOW US TO SPEAK THING TO LIFE TO WATCH THINGS HAPPEN BEFORE OUR EYES AND THE EYES OF OTHERS FAITH IS A POWERFUL THING TO STAND ON USE IT TO THE GLORY OF GOD.

26. THERE ARE TIMES WE COME TO THE STORMS OF LIFE AND THE RAIN FALL IS SO HARD AND WE CANT SEE OUR WAY. BUT WHEN THOSE TIMES COME DON'T STOP JUST SLOW DOWN UNTIL YOU GO THROUGH THE STORM.

27. THINGS MAY NOT BE THE WAY I WANT IT TO BE BUT IT SHALL BE.

28. TAKE YOUR EYES OFF OF MAN AND PUT THEM ON GOD.

29. WHO CAN STOP ME? NO ONE.

Right: being in accordance with what is just, good, or proper.

CHAPTER 4

RIGHT

1. WHEN YOU ARE IN A POSITION TO HELP SOMEONE DO RIGHT BY THEM DON'T LET YOUR ANGER OR FRUSTRATIONS WITH SOMEONE ELSE CAUSE YOU TO MAKE A BAD DECISION FOR THAT PERSON FOR WHOM YOU ARE TO SERVE.

2. TO DO THAT WHICH IS RIGHT YOU MAY FINE YOUR SELF BY YOUR SELF BUT DO IT, THINGS MAY NOT SHOW THEN BUT IT WILL OVER TIME.

3. FROM MY YOUTH I WAS ALWAYS TOLD TO DO THAT WHICH IS RIGHT AND IT WILL PAYOFF WHEN YOU DO THAT WHICH IS RIGHT YOU GAIN FAVOR WITH MAN TRUST WILL BE YOUR FRIEND AND CONVICTION AND YOU WILL FOLLOW IT ALL THE DAYS OF YOU LIFE.

4. DOING WHAT IS RIGHT IS NEVER WRONG, DOING WHAT IS WRONG IS NEVER RIGHT, FOR WE WILL BE REWARDED EITHER WAY.

5. NO MATTER HOW WRONG A PERSON MAY BE AS LONG AS THEY HAVE A BACKER THEY CONTINUE.

6. DO THAT WHICH IS RIGHT UNTO YOUR BROTHER FOR THE PAY OF WRONG WILL COME NO MATTER HOW LONG IT TAKES.

7. TO DO WHAT IS RIGHT IS OFTEN A LONG ROAD TO TRAVEL.

8. RIGHT IS GOOD WHEN IT COMES FROM GOOD. RIGHT IS NO GOOD WHEN IT COMES FROM EVIL.

9. THERE IS A RIGHT WAY AND THERE IS A WRONG WAY. THE RIGHT WAY IS THE MOST DIFFICULT AT THE BEGINNING AND LATER IT BECOME SMOOTH THE WRONG WAY STARTS OUT SMOOTH AND END UP BEING VERY DIFFICULT IN THE END.

10. HOLD TO RIGHT AS A DEAR FRIEND AND IT WILL LEAD YOU TO ALL GOODNESS.

11. IF YOU DON'T FOLLOW THAT WHICH IS RIGHT YOU WILL BECOME A VICTIM OF WRONG.

12. SOME TIMES WE CANT SEE THE GOOD IN DOING THINGS THE RIGHT WAY RIGHT THEN AND THERE BUT TIME WILL SHOW IT.

13. DOING THAT WHICH IS RIGHT CAN LEAVE YOU IN A BAD STATE BUT DO IT ANY HOW.

14. IF YOU DON'T TEACH A CHILD TO DO RIGHT THEY WON'T KNOW WHAT IT MEANS TO DO RIGHT.

15. OVER COME WRONG WITH RIGHT NO MATTER HOW GREAT THE SITUATION OR THE FEEL OF TEMPTATION TO DO IT OVER COME WRONG WITH RIGHT.

16. HAVING A LARGE GATHERING AROUND YOU IN YOUR WRONG DOING DOESN'T MEAN NOR MAKE YOU RIGHT.

17. IT DOESN'T MATTER THE MISTAKES YOU HAVE MADE WHEN YOU COME TO YOURSELF DON'T GO BACK, DO THE RIGHT THING.

18. SO MANY TIMES IN OUR LIFE THING WILL NOT GO RIGHT BUT WE MUST PRESS ON THROUGH IT TO MAKE THINGS HAPPEN.

19. BEING IN A POSITION OF AUTHORITY DOESN'T GIVE YOU THE RIGHT TO TREAT PEOPLE ANY WAY YOU FEEL LIKE. WE ARE ALL UNDER AUTHORITY.

20. YOU CAN'T GO BACK AND CORRECT ALL OF YOUR WRONGS BUT YOU CAN GO FORWARD AND DO THAT WHICH IS RIGHT WITH PURE COURAGE AND STRENGTH.

21. IF YOU HAVE BEEN BLESSED TO HAVE BEEN TAUGHT IN THE RIGHT WAY

BE THANKFUL FOR TO BE TAUGHT IN THE WRONG WAY HAS ITS CONSEQUECENES.

22. JUST BECAUSE YOU MAY BE RIGHT DOESN'T ALWAYS MEAN IT IS THE RIGHT TIME.

23. YOUR WRONG DOING CAN CAUSE A WHOLE LOT OF PAIN NOT ONLY IN YOUR LIFE BUT ALSO IN THE LIVES OF OTHERS AROUND YOU. DO THINGS THE RIGHT WAY. LIFE IS PAINFULL ENOUGH DOING IT THE RIGHT WAY.

24. FOR SO MANY TO SAY I AM SORRY IS NOT WITHIN THEM FOR THEY FEEL IT IS A SIGN OF WEAKNESS NOT THE ATTRIBUTE OF A STRONG LEADER. WELL AS IT MAYBE. BUT IF GOD HIMSELF CAN REPENT WHATS WRONG WITH MAN? WHO IS STRONGER THAN HE?

25. WHY DO WE CONTINUE TO KEEP DOING THE SAME WRONG OVER AND OVER AND OVER AND KEEP LOOKING FOR THINGS TO BE DIFFERENT?

26. IN LIFE THERE ARE THOSE THAT AREN'T THE LEAST BIT CONCERN ABOUT HURTING YOUR FEELINGS AND BELITTLING YOU, HE THAT IS WILLING TO PUT IT OUT SHOULD BE WILLING TO TAKE IT BACK IN. DON'T EAT CROW ALL OF YOUR LIFE.

27. YOU CAN'T EXPECT TO SURROUND YOUR SELF WITH FOOLS AND DO THE RIGHT THINGS COME OUT FROM AMONG THEM.

28. IF WE WERE A BAD EXAMPLE LET US TURN THAT AROUND AND BE A GOOD EXAMPLE SO MANY NEED SOMEONE TO LOOK UP TO.

29. JUST BECAUSE YOU WERE OR HAVE BEEN DOESN'T MEAN YOU HAVE TO ALWAYS BE WHAT YOU WERE.

30. WE EXPECT PEOPLE TO BE THE WAY WE ARE SO MANY TIMES NOT REALIZING THAT THEY ARE NOT. I AM STRONG AND YOU SHOULD BE ALSO.THAT IS NOT ALWAYS THE CASE.

31. THERE ARE THOSE WHO SAY THEY WOULDN'T TAKE THE THINGS THAT I TAKE THAT IS WHY THEY ARE THE WAY THEY ARE AND I AM THE WAY I AM.

32. SOME TIME OTHERS CAN SEE THINGS IN US THAT WE CANT SEE IN OUR SELVES AND WHEN THEY ADDRESS THE ISSUE WE GET ANGRY.

33. PEOPLE THAT HAVE THINGS ON THERE MIND MANY TIMES AND IT IS OVER FLOWING IN THEM BUT DON'T HAVE THE NERVE TO SPEAK IT OUT MANY TIME WOULD DRINK JUST ENOUGH LIQUOR TO SAY WHAT THEY HAVE TO SAY AND BLAME THE LIQUOR.

34. IF YOU NEED ME CALL ME IS SO EASY TO SAY. YOU CALL ONE TIME TO MANY AND THEY GET UPSET. DON'T SAY IT IF YOU DON'T MEAN IT SOMEONE MAY TAKE YOU UP ON IT.

35. WHEN YOU ASK YOUR PARENTS TO TRUST YOU. DON'T DISAPPOINT THEM IT MAY NOT GO GOOD FOR YOU THE NEXT TIME YOU ASK.

36. PEOPLE MAY NOT COMMENT YOU ON HOW YOU CARRY YOURSELF UNTIL YEARS LATER.

37. YOU PUT TO MUCH PRESSURE ON STEEL YOU WILL BEND IT. DON'T OVER LOAD YOURSELF.

38. WHEN YOU STAND UP FOR WHAT IS RIGHT ENEMIES WILL COME OUT OF THE WOOD WORKS.

39. SOMEONE HAVE TO MAKE THE SACRIFICE IN ORDER FOR OTHER TO BENEFIT.

40. YOU MAY HAVE TO UPSET THE WHOLE WORLD IN ORDER FOR JUSTICE TO PREVAIL.

41. JUSTICE FOR SOME MAY NOT BE JUSTICE FOR ALL.

42. THERE ARE SO MANY THAT ARE READY TO DO AND SAY THINGS WHEN IT DOSEN,T COUNT AND WHEN IT REALLY MATTERS THEY BECOME SILENT.

43. DOING THINGS WRONG IN PRIVATE WILL SOONER OR LATER COME OUT IN THE OPEN.

44. THE TONGUE CAN CAUSE SO MUCH TROUBLE AND WHEN IT IS FINISH IT HIDE BEHIND THE TOOTH.

45. DON'T BE SPITEFUL TO ME JUST BECAUSE YOU DESPISE SOMEONE AND I DON'T.

46. JUST BECAUSE YOU DON'T FEEL LIKE DOING SOMETHING THAT IS IMPORTANT DON'T MEAN JUST SIT THERE, GET STARTED AND YOUR FEELINGS WILL CHANGE.

47. NO MATTER HOW LONG IT TAKES. IF YOU DO RIGHT YOU WILL COME OUT OF TROUBLE.

48. STOP TRYING TO DO THINGS RIGHT AND GOING THE WRONG WAY OF DOING IT.

49. THE THINGS THAT MAKES US FEEL GOOD SOMETIMES ARE THE MAIN THINGS WE SHOULD GET RID OF EVERYTHING THAT MAKES US FEEL GOOD ISNT ALWAYS GOOD FOR US.

50. STOP TRYING TO HOLD ON TO THINGS YOU KNOW YOU NEED TO GET RID OF.

51. SOMETIME THE THINGS WE GO THROUGH MAY SEEM LIKE A WASTE BUT IT ISN'T.

52. EXCEPT YOU GO THROUGH THINGS YOU WON'T HAVE THE EXPERIENCE TO CHALLENGE ANYTHING.

53. LEARN FROM HARD LESSONS AND EASY ONES TOO, THEY ARE YOUR TEACHER.

54. DON'T TAKE ANYTHING FOR A JOKE IN THE END IT WILL COME BACK TO YOU.

Love: a feeling of warm personal attachment or deep affection, as for a parent, child, or friend.

CHAPTER 5

LOVE

1. IF YOU LOVE ME AND I LOVE YOU WE WILL BUILD ON EACH OTHER STRENGTH AND STRENGTHEN EACH OTHER WEAKNESS.

2. LOVE ONLY LEADS TO REWARDS IT MAY TAKE TIME TO GROW.PLANTED PROPERLY IT WILL PRODUCE ABUNDANCE.

3. LOVE IS STRONG ENOUGH TO DEFEAT ANYTHING THAT COMES AGAINST IT YOU CANT DEFEAT TRUE LOVE.

4. HAVING LOVE IN A RELATIONSHIP WITHOUT UNDERSTANDING AND KNOWLEDGE CAN SOONER OR LATER HAVE YOU IN LOVE WITH EACH OTHER BUT YOU WILL NOT BE TOGETHER.

5. LOVE GOES BEYOND FEELINGS IT CAUSES YOU TO FORGIVE THE THINGS WE CONSIDER UNFORGIVEABLE.

6. IF YOU TRULY LOVE SOME ONE YOU WILL LEARN TO DEAL WITH UNDERSTANDING AND PATIENCE.

7. SENDING OUT YOUR LOVE DOESN'T MEAN YOU WILL ALWAYS GET IT BACK THERE ARE THOSE THAT WILL DESPISE YOU JUST BECAUSE OF WHO YOU ARE BUT KEEP SENDING IT OUT THEY WILL COME TO SHAME ONE DAY.

8. SPEAK LOVE FROM YOUR HEART NOT YOUR LIPS.

9. LOVE WILL CAUSE YOU TO WORK TOGETHER FOR ALL OF THE GOALS IN YOU'RE LIFE.

10. YOU MAY NOT ALWAYS FEEL LOVE BUT WHEN IT IS NEEDED IT SHOWS UP.

11. ONE SIDED LOVE CAN COME WITH MANY DAYS OF TEARS GIVING LOVE DOESN'T MEAN YOU WILL ALWAYS GET LOVE.

12. LOVE SHOULD BE IN OUR HEART TO ALL MAN AND WHEN IT IS APART OF US WE CAN ALL BECOME APART OF EACH OTHER.

13. THERE IS MUCH STRENGTH IN LOVE.

14. TRUE LOVE WILL BRING US PEACE BEYOND ANYTHING WE CAN IMAGINE OR GO THROUGH.

15. LOVE IS A GREAT MEDICINE IT CURES ALL THINGS WITH THE RIGHT DOSAGE AND TIME.

16. IF THE LOVE OF GOD DWELLS IN YOU. YOU WILL FOR GIVE NO MATTER WHAT.

17. IF YOU LOVE ME WE WILL SUFFER TOGETHER UNTIL EVERYTHING BLOWS OVER.

18. AFTER GOING THROUGH THE TEST OF TIME LOVE WILL GIVE YOU ALL THINGS.

19. BECAUSE OF THE LOVE THAT I HAVE FOR YOU WHEN EVER I SEE YOU I CAN KEEP FROM SMILING.

20. WHEN A MAN AND A WOMAN FALLS IN LOVE IT GOES FAR BEYOND PHYSICAL ATTRACTION LOOKS MY NOT LAST FOR EVER BUT TRUE LOVE WILL.

21. TWO PEOPLE IN LOVE FIGHT THINGS OUT TOGETHER NO MATTER HOW STRONG THE OPPRESSOR.

22. BEING IN LOVE AND LOVED BY YOUR MATE IS ONE OF THE GREATEST EXPERINCE WE CAN HAVE IN THIS LIFE WHEN MONEY FAIL FRIENDS GO AWAY AND FAMILY FORSAKE WHEN YOU LOOK AROUND THE ONE YOU LOVE IS STILL STANDING THERE SAYING WE CAN MAKE IT. WE DID IT BEFORE WE CAN DO IT AGAIN.

hum·ble

[huhm-buhl, uhm-] Show IPA adjective, -bler, -blest, verb, -bled, -bling.

adjective

1. not proud or arrogant; modest: to be humble although successful.

CHAPTER 6

HUMBLE

1. THE SPIRIT OF THE HUMBLE BRINGTH MUCH, THE GREED OF THE ARROGANT BRINGTH PAIN.

2. THERE ARE MANY THAT HAVE SAID NO ONE EVER GIVEN ME ANYTHING. NOT KNOWING THAT THEY HAVE BEEN CHOSEN AMONG THE FEW TO BE A GIVER OF THOSE WHO WAS'NT AS BLESSED AND INSTED OF DOING THE RIGHT THING THEY JUST KEEP INFLICTING PAIN UPON THE POOR.BUT AS A MAN SEW SO SHALL HE REAP.

3. WE ARE SO QUICK TO PUT OTHERS DOWN WHEN IT SEEMS TO BE GOING WELL WITH US NOT THINKING THAT WE ARE JUST ONE STEP AWAY FROM THE SAME TROUBLE.

4. DON'T DO THINGS JUST TO LOOK BIG AND BE SEEN OF MAN IT IS OF NO PROFIT.

5. THE ONE WHOM LOWER HIMSELF BEFORE GOD WILL RISE ABOVE ALL.

6. THE HUMBLE WILL APOLOGIZE; THE ARROGANT AND HIGH MINDED WILL NOT.

7. THE HUMBLE WILL SUBMIT THE FOOLISH GOES ON UNTO DESTRUCTION.

8. IT TAKES A DISASTER FOR PEOPLE TO REALIZE THAT POWER IS NOT IN MONEY WHEN A NATURAL DISASTER COME THE RICH AND POOR ARE IN THE SAME LINE FOR FOOD AND WATER AND ALL OTHER ESSENTIALS THE ONLY POWER THERE IS OF GOD IS AND THERE ARE THOSE TIMES WHEN HE HAVE TO REMIND US ALL OF THAT.

9. THE HUMBLE WILL RISE AND THE ARROGANT WILL SURELY FALL. NO MATTER HOW LONG IT TAKES JUST WAIT.

10. THE HUMBLE HAVE PATIENCE FOR HE KNOWS HIS DAY WILL COME.

11. HUMBLE PEOPLE LEARN TO ENDURE ALL THINGS.

12. WHEN WE LEARN TO REDUCE OUR POWER GOD WILL GIVE US ALL POWER.

13. PRIDE HAS BROUGHT MISERY IN THE LIVES OF MANY.

14. COMPLAINING HAVE NO PLACE IN THE HOUSE OF THE HUMBLE.

15. DON'T LET ANYONE TALK YOU OUT OF BEING HUMBLE AND TURN THE WRATH OF GOD UPON YOU.

16. ONE OF THE QUICKEST WAYS TO DESTRUCTION IS TO BE FOOLISH.

17. WE FIND IT HARD TO TOLERATE THE MISTAKES OF OTHERS BUT WHEN IT HAPPENS TO US WE EXPECT EVERYONE TO BE TOLERANT OF US.

18. THANK YOU IS SUCH A POLITE THING TO SAY IT SHOWS THE FACT THAT YOU APPRECIATE WHAT HAVE BEEN GIVE TO YOU.AND THAT YOU ARE GRATEFUL FOR THE THINGS YOU HAVE RECEIVED, JUST TO WAKE UP IN THE MORNING AND SAY THANK YOU LORD FOR ANOTHER DAY SHOWS GOD YOUR APPRECIATION FOR ALLOWING YOU TO WAKE UP ONE MORE TIME OR SAY THANKS FOR SOMEONE HELPING IN TIME OF NEED THANK YOU MAY NOT SOUND LIKE MUCH BUT IT CAN MAKE A DIFFRENCE IN YOU RECEIVING SOMETHING FROM SOMEONE EVER AGAIN.

19. I WOULD RATHER SAY ONE WORD TO ENCOURAGE A MAN THAN TO SAY A THOUSAND AND DISCOURAGE HIM.

20. THERE IS NOTHING WRONG WITH BEING POOR IT IS JUST SO INCONVENIENT.

21. HUMBLENESS IS THE NATURE OF A CHILD.

22. ASKING FOR HELP DOESN'T BELITTLE A MAN IT JUST SHOWS THAT HE NEEDS HELP, IN TROUBLE WE NEED EACH OTHER.

23. SO MANY TIMES HUNGER CAN SHUT DOWN A WHOLE LOT OF COMPLAINTS WE HAVE BEEN SO USE OF HAVING THE WHOLE LOAF AND NOT REALIZEING TROUBLE IS JUST A FLICK AWAY. WHEN HUMBLE TIMES COME WE FEEL JUST AS GOOD WITH THE HALF LOAF THAN WE DID WITH THE WHOLE LOAF.

24. WHY DO WE HAVE TO WAIT FOR TROUBLE TO COME AND HUMBLE US?

25. A HUMBLE PERSON IS A CONTENTED PERSON.

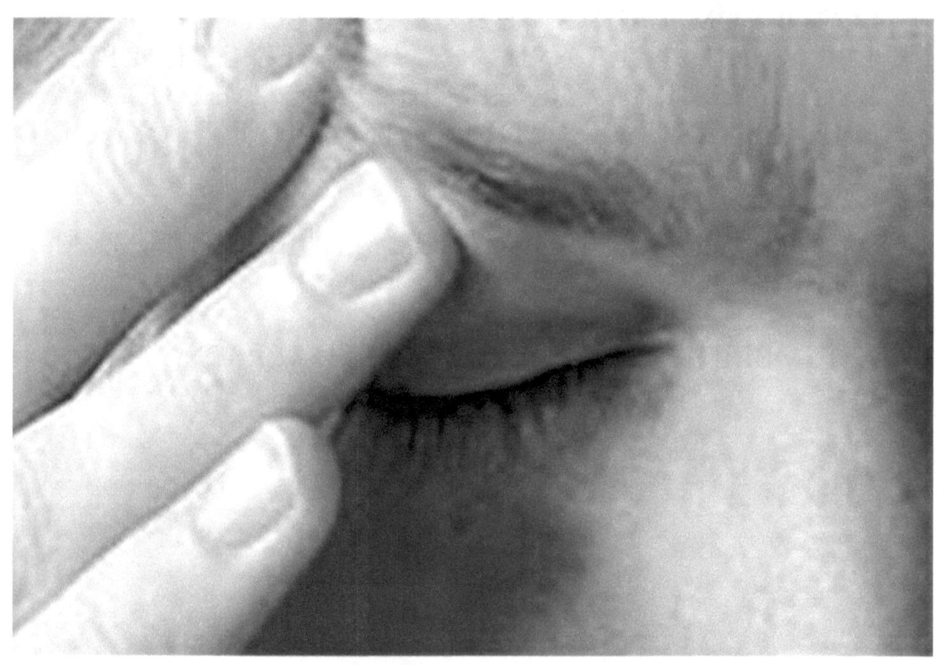

PAIN: physical suffering or distress, as due to injury, illness, etc

CHAPTER 7
PAIN

1. PAIN HELPS US SEEK A CURE.

2. EASY COMES AFTER YEARS GOING THROUGH AND THEN IT GETS BETTER.

3. ONE THING ABOUT THE BODY YOU INJURE ONE PART AND THE WHOLE BODY FEEL IT.

4. THERE ARE SO MANY PAINFUL THINGS WE GO THROUGH IN LIFE TO KEEP US FROM MAKING A VERY BIG MISTAKE.

5. DONT EVER REJOICE OVER SOMEONES FAILURE OR FALL.

6. WHEN WE DO THE RIGHT THINGS TO OTHERS PAIN DISSIPATE.

7. SAVE YOURSELF FROM PAIN LEARN TO LISTEN.

8. THE SAME PAIN YOU INFLICT TO OTHERS WILL FIND ITS WAY BACK TO YOU.

PARENT: to be or act as parent of: to parent children with both love and discipline.

CHAPTER 8

PARENT

1. YOU MUST TEACH YOUR CHILDREN TO DO GOOD OR THEY WONT KNOW.

2. YOUR PARENTS KNOWS WHAT YOU WILL DO EVEN BEFORE YOU DO IT. HOW IS THAT SO YOU SAY, THEY WERE ONCE IN YOUR SHOES.

3. A CHILD CAN NOT FOOL GOOD PARENTS THEY JUST HUMOR THEM SELVES WHEN THEY THINK SO.

4. PARENTS MAY NOT ALWAYS BE RIGHT IN YOUR SIGHT BUT THEY ARE STILL THE PARENTS.

5. BEING A TEENAGER WE OFTIME THINK WE ARE SO SMART AND OUR PARENTS SO DUMB BUT AS WE GET OLDER WE REALIZE JUST HOW DUMB WE WERE AND HOW SMART OUR PARENTS ARE.

6. PARENTS ARE TEACHERS OF A NEW GENERATION A GENERATION THAT NEED INSTRUCTIONS FROM THE DAY THEY BEGIN TO UNDERSTAND.

7. STRENGTH AND LEADERSHIP NEVER BACKING DOWN, CARING PROTECTOR PROVIDER, MAN OF FAITH, LOVE. THE MAN IN MY LIFE ALLOWED ME TO SEE KNOW AND UNDERSTAND THESE THINGS SO THAT I CAN DO THE SAME WITH MY OWN CHILDREN THAT MAN IS MY FATHER.

8. GOOD HOME TRAINING IS THE PATHWAY TO BEING TRAINED FOR EVERYTHING ELSE IN LIFE A GIFT THAT GOES FROM GENERATION TO GENERATION. DON'T LEAVE HOME WITH OUT IT. IT IS ONE TRAIT THAT WILL ABIDE FOR EVER WHEN ADMINISTERED PROPERLY.

9. I AM NOT YOUR BUDDY OR PAL I AM YOUR MOTHER OR YOU'RE FATHER. I MAY NOT BE THE COOLEST OR SPEAK THE DIFFERENT SLANGS NOR BE THE HIPPEST PARENT

ON THE BLOCK. BUT I WILL BE THE ONE TO MAKE SURE YOU GROW INTO A RESPONSIBLE WOMAN OR MAN.

10. PARENTS KEEP YOUR PAST LIFE TO YOUR SELF CHILDREN NEED TO KNOW ONLY WHAT THEY NEED TO KNOW. LET YOUR EXPERIENCES DIRECT THEM.

11. LOVE YOUR PARENTS FOR YOU ONLY GET ONE SET.

12. A CHILD MAY FIND MANY THINGS THERE PARENTS WOULD HAVE THEM TO DO, AS BEING A HARDSHIP BECAUSE THEY ARE A CHILD AND LACK MUCH UNDERSTANDING AND EXPERIENCE.

13. A GOOD FATHER TAKES TIME FOR HIS FAMILY HELPS OUT AROUND THE HOUSE AND DO THE NECCESSARY THINGS TO PROMOTE PEACE.

14. FOR A MAN TO CALL HIMSELF A MAN AND NOT BE IN CONTROL OF HIS HOUSE HE NEEDS TO STOP CALLING HIMSELF A MAN AND FIND OUT WHAT A MAN IS.

15. THE FIRST THIRTY DAYSOF A NEW BORN BEING AT HOME IS VERY TRYING.

16. A GOOD CHILD BRINGS PRIDE AND JOY TO THERE PARENTS LIKE NOTING ELSE COULD.

17. THERE IS A SPECIAL CONNECTION BETWEEN FATHERS AND THERE DAUGHTERS IF YOU WANT TO LIVE A LONG AND PAIN FREE LIFE DON'T MESS WITH HIS DAUGHTERS.

18. YOUR CHILDREN ARE TO BE A BLESSING TO YOU. MANY TIME THEY BECOME A CURSE TO YOU BECAUSE. YOU ARE MORE INTO YOURSELF THAN YOU CHILDREN.

19. IT DOESN'T MATTER WHAT ANYONE HAVE TO SAY I HAVE TO RAISE THIS CHILD.

20. I DON'T NEED THE POLICE TO RAISE MY CHILDREN I CAN DO IT THROUGH THE GRACE OF GOD.

21. MY CHILD WILL NOT BE A STATISTIC.

22. YOU CAN RAISE YOUR CHILD THE WAY YOU WANT TO BUT I WILL RAISE MINE THE WAY THEY OUGHT TO BE RAISED.

23. BEING A STRICK PARENT WITH THE RIGHT UNDERSTANDING CAN SAVE YOU A WORLD OF PAIN LATER.

24. CORRECTING A CHILD IS ONE THING. ABUSING THEM IS ANOTHER CORRECTION SHOULD NEVER BE TAKEN AWAY FROM A CHILD FOR WITHOUT IT THEY BECOME UNRULY.

25. CHILDREN THAT HAVE BEEN RAISED UP RIGHT WILL ONE DAY COME BACK AND THANK YOU.

26. BE CAREFUL WHAT YOU DO AND SAY AROUND YOUR CHILDREN FOR A CHILD DON'T FORGET

27. DON'T SAY WHAT YOUR CHILD WILL NOT DO. THEY HAVE AWAY OF DISSAPOINTING YOU SOMETIMES.

28. A FATHER OR A MOTHER LOVE CAN NOT BE MEASURED WITH WORDS IT HAVE A PRICE THAT IS MORE VALUABLE THAN ANY PRECIOUS STONE.

29. PARENTS MUST WORK TOGETHER WHEN BRINGING UP THERE CHILDREN MAMA SAY "NO DADDY SAID NO" DADDY SAY "NO MAMA SAID NO". OTHER WISE YOUR CHILDREN WILL PLAY YOU AGAINST EACH OTHER.

30. DON'T ALLOW YOUR OLDER CHILD TO DO SOMETHING THAT YOU DON'T WANT THE YOUNGER SIBLING TO DO FOR IN DOING SO THEY WILL BRING IT UP AGAIN.WHEN

YOU TELL THEM NOT TO DO THE SAME THING THAT THE OTHER DID.

31. EVERYTHING IS NOT ALWAYS GOING TO BE WELL WITH YOU BUT TAKE IT IN STRIDE.

32. HAPPIENESS BETWEEN THE PARENTS IS AND ENCOURAGEMENT TO THEIR CHILDREN AT ANY AGE.

33. NO PARENT SHOULD ALLOW ANY BAD INFLUNCES TO COME INTO THEIR HOME AND RUIN THERE CHILDREN.

MARRIAGE: the social institution under which a man and woman establish their decision to live as husband and wife by legal commitments, religious ceremonies, etc.

CHAPTER 9

MARRIAGE

1. A PERSON THAT IS NOT CONTENT IN ANYWAY AND IS VERY UNSETTLED MAY BE BARKING UP THE WRONG TREE AS FAR AS MARRIAGE IS CONCERN.

2. MARRIED PEOPLE AND SINGLE PEOPLE DON'T NEED TO HANG OUT TOGETHER.

3. MARRIAGE IS NOT MADE TO GROW APART BUT TOGETHER OUTSIDE INFULENCES AND JEALOUSY OF OTHERS CAN STUNT THE GROWTH OF A HEALTHY RELATIONSHIP.

4. A GOOD MARRIAGE IS WORTH TELLING THE WORLD ABOUT.

5. MARRIED PEOPLE NEED TO CHOOSE THERE FRIENDS CAREFULLY.

6. DON'T BE RUSHED INTO MARRIAGE THIS IS ONE OF MOST IMPORTANT DECISION THAT YOU WILL MAKE IN YOUR LIFE TIME THAT WILL LAST THE REST OF YOUR LIFE CHOOSE YOUR COMPANION WITH MUCH CARE.

7. DONT LET YOURSELF GO JUST BECAUSE YOU ARE MARRIED MAINTAIN YOURSELF.

8. WE SHOULD NOT ALLOW PROBLEMS TO CREATE A DEAF EAR OR SILENT TONGUE IN OUR RELATIONSHIP WE WILL HAVE PROBLEMS BUT WE MUST TALK.

9. NEVER ALLOW YOUR RELATIONSHIP TO BECOME A TASK FOR EITHER OF YOU.

10. BEING KIND, POLITE AND MEETING EACH OTHER NEEDS HOLDS A RELATIONSHIP TOGETHER.

11. YOU ARE THERE FOR THE NEEDS OF EACH OTHER DON'T ALLOW YOURSELF TO FORSAKE OUR FORGET TO MEET THE NEEDS OF EACH OTHER A HUNGRY PERSON

CONTINUE TO EAT A FULL PERSON WANT EAT ANYMORE NO MATTER HOW GOOD THE MEAL MAY LOOK.

12. AHUSBANDANDWIFEMUSTTAKETIMEFOREACHOTHER AND NOT ALLOW THE FLAME TO GO OUT BECAUSE OF CIRCUMSTANCES.

13. YOU START A MARRIAGE WITH JUST THE TWO OF YOU. AND AS TIME GOES BY CHILDREN COME ALONG AND YOU FIND YOURSELF CAREING FOR THEM MORE THAN FOR EACH OTHER. BUT KEEP IN MIND THEY WILL GROW UP AND LEAVE AND THE TWO OF YOU WILL BE AS YOU WERE IN THE BEGINNING BUT ONLY WITH THE BLESSIED FRUITS OF LOVING CHILDRENS.

14. IT WILL TAKE YEARS FOR YOU TO FINALLY UNDERSTAND EACH OTHER IN A MARRAGE DON'T BE SO QUICK TO GIVE UP.

15. NEVER BRING A THIRD PARTY INTO YOUR MARRIAGE IT ISNT WISE.

16. DONT LET THE PAIN AND JEALOUSY OF OTHER CAUSE YOU TO MAKE A DUMB AND SILLY MISTAKES AND LEAVE HOME THINKING YOU WILL COME UPON GREENER PASTURE AND WHEN YOU GET THERE ALL YOU FINE IS A FIELD FILLED WITH PATCHS AND HOLES.

17. A MARRIED MAN HAVING FEMALE FRIENDS OR A MARRIED WOMAN HAVING MALE FRIENDS MAY BE ASKING FOR TROUBLE, AVOID SUCH THINGS.

18. AS LONG AS THERE IS NO ABUSE. PROBLEMS IN YOUR RELATIONSHIP SHOULD BE WORKED OUT BETWEEN THE TWO OF YOU.AND IF IT IS MORE THAN YOU THINK YOU COULD HANDLE ALONG GET HELP. JUST LEAVE FRIENDS OUT.THERE ADVICE CAN CAUSE MORE PROBLEMS THAN WHAT IT IS WORTH.

19. WHEN YOU ARE MARRIED DO NOT GO LOOKING FOR ANOTHER PARTNER HAVE FAITH IN EACH OTHER.

20. THERE ARE THINGS A HUSBAND OR A WIFE WILL PUT UP WITH THAT BOYFRIEND OR GIRLFRIEND WON'T.

21. WHEN A HUSBAND OR A WIFE TELL THEIR COMPANION SOMETHING THAT MAY BE HARD TO SWALLOW HE OR SHE ARE NOT SAYING IT TO START TROUBLE BUT FOR THE OTHER TO PAY ATTENTION TO WHAT THEY ARE DOING.

22. IN A MARRIAGE WE SHOULD BE ABLE TO HAVE SOUND DISCUSSIONS NO MATTER HOW UNCOMFORTABLE IT MAY SEEM TO BE OR CAUSE US TO FEEL IT IS HEALTHY.

23. WHEN YOU ARE MARRIED LEARN TO BE A GOOD LISTENER.

24. A HUSBAND AND WIFE MAY HAVE A SECRET IT DOESN'T MEAN THE END OF THEIR MARRIAGE.

25. WILL MY WIFE AND I HAVE SOME BAD DISAGREEMENTS ALONG THE WAY DOES A DOG HAVE TEETH.

26. THE ONLY WAY YOUR MARRIAGE WILL LAST THE TEST OF TIME IS IF YOU BOTH WANT IT TO. IF YOU SET YOUR SIGHTS ON SOMEONE ELSE IT WILL BE VERY DIFFICULT TO DO SO.

27. YOU LOOKED GOOD ENOUGH TO GET EACH OTHER ATTENTION WHAT MAKE YOU THINK YOU WANT DRAW THE ATTENTION OF OTHERS STAND TOGETHER AND KEEP EACH OTHER ATTENTION AND THE ADVERSARY WANT STAND A CHANCE.

28. IN A MARRIAGE A HUSBAND IS THERE TO PROTECT HIS WIFE JUST AS SHE IS THERE TO PROTECT HIM.

29. GET PLEASURE IN PRAISING EACH OTHER RATHER THAN KNOCKING EACH OTHER DOWN.

30. IF YOU BLAME YOUR WIFE FOR EVERYTHING AND SHE DO THE SAME TO YOU WHO IS TO BLAME? A LITTLE LEVEL WILL THE WHOLE LUMP. WORK THINGS OUT.

31. DON'T CREATE PROBLEMS WHEN THERE ISNT ANY BE PATIENCE WITH EACH OTHER.

32. LACK OF ATTENTION CAN CAUSE YOU TO START THINKING DIFFRENTLY.

33. PLUM THE LINE GET THINGS STRAIGHT, TIME WILL BRING CHANGES AS YOU AGE BE THERE FOR HIM BE THERE FOR HER.

34. PROBLEMS WILL COME BETWEEN THE TWO OF YOU DON'T ALLOW ANGER TO SET IN,IN SUCH AWAY THAT YOU DON'T HEAR EACH OTHER AND NOT WORK OUT A WORKABLE PROBLEM. YOU CAN WORK PAST YOUR PROBLEM.

35. LISTEN MORE ARGUE LESS.

36. BIG MISTAKES ARE MADE WHEN WE STAY ANGRY WITH EACH OTHER.

37. BEING CAREER MINDED IS ONE THING, BUT DON'T LET IT COME IN BETWEEN YOUR RELATIONSHIP MAKE TIME FOR EACH OTHER.

38. MARRIAGE IS US NOT YOU AND ME.

39. DON'T EVER EMBARRASS YOUR HUSBAND OR WIFE OUT IN THE PUBLIC IF YOU HAVE A DIFFERENCE OF OPINION WAIT UNTIL YOU HAVE YOUR PRIVATE TIME AND WORK THINGS OUT IN PEACE.

40. DON'T BELITTLE EACH OTHER PUBLICLY OR PRIVATELY IT ISN'T WISE.

41. LEARN HOW TO BE HUMBLE EACH TO THE OTHER AND WATCH YOUR MARRIAGE GROW.

42. YOU ARE THE MAN OF THE HOUSE BE THE MAN OF THE HOUSE.YOUR THE WOMAN OF THE HOUSE BE THE WOMAN OF THE HOUSE.

43. IT IS ALRIGHT TO SPEND SOME TIME AWAY FROM EACH OTHER, JUST DON'T LEAVE TO MUCH SPACE IN BETWEEN EACH OTHER FOR LONG SOMETHING ELSE MAY FILL THE GAP.

The quality of being patient, as the bearing of provocation, annoyance, misfortune, or pain, without complaint, loss of temper, irritation, or the like.

CHAPTER 10

PATIENCE

1. ONE OF THE QUICKEST WAY TO DESTRUCTION IS TO BE IMPATIENCE AND DO FOOLISH THINGS.

2. WE CAN GIVE UP ON OTHERS SO QUICKLY THAT LOOK AS THOUGH THEY AREN'T GOING ANY WHERE AND LATER FIND OUT THEY ENDED UP BEING MORE SUCCESSFUL THAN THE ONES THAT GAVE UP ON THEM.

3. BEING IMPATIENT CAN CAUSE YOU TO WALK AWAY FROM SUCCESS IT MY HAVE NO SIGN OF BEING ANYTHING BUT IT WAS ALL THE TIME.

4. BIG DIVIDENDS ARE PAYED IN THE END WITH PATIENCE IT MIGHT NOT COME EASY BUT YOUR PATIENCE WILL PAY OFF IN THE END.

5. WHILE THE GRASS IS GROWING THE COW IS STARVING.

6. WE MAY SUFFER FOR A WHILE AND EVEN THOUGH IT MAY SEEM LIKE THE WINTER OF OUR LIFE WON'T PASS, BUT KEEP IN MIND THAT AFTER WINTER COMES SPRING.

7. A PERSON OF GREAT PATIENCE AND HOPE IS A STRONG PERSON.

8. MANY CAN NOT SEE YOU AS YOU ARE FOR THE FAILURES YOU HAVE HAD IN YOUR QUEST FOR GREATNESS BUT GOD CAN.

9. TO LOOK AT THE WORK OF A CRAFTMAN IS AND AMAZING THING BUT TO BECOME ONE REQUIRES SO MUCH PATIENCE AND WORK.

10. TO BE SOMEONE IN THE CAPACITY TO SERVE OTHERS AND LACK PATIENCE YOU CAN BE COME A CALLUS RATHER THAN A HELP.

11. JUST BECAUSE YOU GO THROUGH TOUGH THINGS SEEMLY WITH NO END IN SIGHT DOSEN'T MEAN THAT THERE IS NO END.

12. GIVING UP COMES TO MIND SO MANY TIMES WHEN CONTINUED PRESSURE IS PLACED UPON US BUT PRESSURE ONLY BRINGS OUT THE GOOD LOCKED UP ON THE INSIDE OF US.

13. WE CAN GET OVER SORROWS, PAIN, POVERTY, ANGER AND HATE WITH TIME.

14. THE BODY CAN HEAL ITSELF OVER TIME AND WITH TIME ALL OF OUR PROBLEMS CAN BE FIXED.

15. KEEP GOING THE BETTER PART OF YOUR LIFE IS YET TO COME.

16. WE WILL HAVE DELAYS IN LIFE WAIT PATIENTLY.

17. KEEP ON LIVING YOU WILL UNDERSTAND LATER ON IN LIFE.

18. THE PATHWAY FOR SOME WILL BE LONGER THAN OTHERS. AND SOME WILL REACH THERE DESTINATION SOONER, DON'T BE DISTRACTED.

19. YOU MAY GET THERE BEFORE I DO BUT I WILL GET THERE.

20. SO MANY OF US WILL HAVE OUR WORLD TURNED UPSIDE DOWN IT DOSEN'T MATTER WHETHER WE DID SOMETHING OR WHETHER WE DIDN'T, BUT WE MUST TAKE IT WITH PATIENCE TO WORK THINGS OUT WHEN IT HAPPENS.

21. TROUBLE COMES AND WE SEEM TO THINK IT WILL LAST FOR EVER BUT IT WON'T.

22. DOUBT CAN CAUSE YOU TO PROLONG YOUR SUFFERING.

23. BEING IMPATIENCE CAN PUT YOU IN A FAR WORST POSITION. THAT WOULD REQUIRE MORE PATIENCE THAN IT WOULD HAVE BEEN FROM THE BEGINNING.

24. WE ALL HAVE THE ABILITY TO BE SUCCESSFUL BUT TO THINK IT HAPPENS OVERNIGHT CAN BRING A LOT OF DISAPPOINTMENT.

25. AFTER GOING THROUGH FOR A SEASON THE JOYS OF IT ALL WILL SPEAK FOR IT'S SELF.

26. IT IS NOT WHAT YOU ARE GOING THROUGH THAT MAKES YOU GO ON BUT WHAT YOU HAVE PREDESTIN.

27. A FARMER IS A GOOD EXAMPLE OF PATIENCE THEY PLANT THE SEED AND WAIT FOR THE RESULTS. WE ALL MUST FOLLOW SUCH A PATTERN FOR WE ALL PLANT OUR SEED BUT NOW WE WILL HAVE TO WAIT ON THE RESULTS.

28. IF YOU DON'T COMPLETE IT TODAY LORD WILLING THERE WILL BE TOMORROW.

29. WAITING ON AND ANSWER FOR A LONG PERIOD OF TIME CAN TAKE A TOLL. BUT TO RECEIVE THE ANSWER THAT YOU HAVE BEEN WAITING ON WILL PAY FOR IT ALL.

30. WAITING ON THE RESULTS OF GOOD TAKE TIME. BUT WAIT ON IT THE REWARDS ARE GREAT. GOOD THINGS COMES TO THOSE THAT WAIT.

The state or quality of being obedient.

The act or practice of obeying; dutiful or submissive compliance

CHAPTER 11
OBEDIENCE

1. IF MY WILL DOSENT COMPLY WITH THE WILL OF GOD IT IS WORTHLESS.

2. OBEDIENCE SAVES PAIN, PREVENTS DEATH, BRINGETH PROSPERTY, FAVOR

3. WE CAN OBEY THE ORDERS OF MAN BUT WHEN IT COMES TO GOD WE CAN BE VERY DISOBEDIENCE.

4. BEING OBEDIENT IS NOT A TASK IT IS A WAY TO YOUR BLESSINGS.

5. AN OBEDIENT PERSON OBSEVE RIGHT AND FOLLOW IT. JUST AS A DISOBEDIENT PERSON DON'T FOLLOW AND WONDER WHY ALL THING KEEP FALLING UPON THEM.

6. EVERYTIME YOU MAKE A STEP FORWARD YOU TAKE TEN BACK STOP FIGHTING WITH YOURSELF ONLY OBEY.

7. WE ALL MUST OBEY SOMEONE WHETHER WE LIKE IT OR NOT, OBEDIENCE IS A PART OF ALL OF OUR LIVES MALE OR FEMALE IT DOSEN'T DISCRIMINATE.

8. ONLY A FOOLISH PERSON WOULD HAVE YOU TO THINK THAT BEING OBEDIENT IS INCORRECT BUT THEY ALWAYS WANT SOMEONE TO OBEY THEM.

9. THERE IS NO HARDSHIP IN OBEDIENCE. OUR SELFISH PRIDE WOULD MAKE US THINK SO AND MANY TIMES WE REFUSE AND SUFFER.

10. BEING OBEDIENT SAVE TIME AND RESOURCES.

MATTHEW 18:21-22
Then came Peter to him, and said, Lord, how oft though shall my brother sin against me, and I forgive him? Till seven times? Jesus saith unto him, I say not unto thee, Until seven times but, Until seventy times seven.

CHAPTER 12

FORGIVENESS

1. PEOPLE LACKING IN UNDERSTANDING AND EXPERIENCE CAN BE VERY UNFORGIVING AND GREAT IN MISCHIEF.

2. IF YOU NEVER GO THROUGH ANYTHING YOU KNOW NOTHING BUT THE SURFACE OF ALL THINGS.

3. SOMEONE FALL IS NOT TOTAL ANNIHILATION OF THAT PERSON THE SAME GOD THAT SHOWS MERCY AND GIVES HIS GRACE IS WILLING TO DO IT AGAIN.

4. NEVER LET YOUR LACK OF UNDERSTANDING BRING COMPLICATIONS IN LIVES OF OTHERS.

5. TO PUNISH SOMEONE CONTINUALLY AFTER THEY HAVE BEEN FORGIVE OF THERE DEEDS YOU BECOME THE FALLEN AND THEY THE FORGIVEN.

6. LOOKING DOWN ON ME NOW WITH AND UNFORGIVING HEART WILL ONE DAY HAVE EVERYONE LOOKING AT YOU.

7. ONLY A FOOL WANT FORGIVE IT IS TO HIGH FOR THEM TO REACH.

8. EVEN THOUGH THE PAIN MAY BE HARD TO BEAR WE MUST FORGIVE AND NOT ALLOW FEELING TO MAKE A FOOLISH PERSON OUT OF US AT A LATER DATE.

9. HOW CAN YOU NOT FORGIVE AND YOU HAVE SHORT COMINGS YOURSELF.

10. ONCE YOU HAVE BEEN FORGIVEN DON'T GO BACK TO THE SAMETHING.

11. FORGIVE AND LET GO ONLY THE UNDERTAKER SHOULD HANDLE THE DEAD.

12. NO ONE HAVE THE RIGHT TO HOLD ANYTHING OVER YOUR HEAD ONCE YOU HAVE BEEN FORGIVEN.

13. FORGIVENESS ISN'T SOMETHING WE DO WHEN WE GET READY BUT SOMETHING WE DO FOR IT IS RIGHT AND WE OUR SELVES CANT BE FORGIVEN UNLESS WE FORGIVE OTHERS.

14. INSTEAD OF TURNING OVER A NEW LEAF TAKE THE SAMEONE AND START ERASING.

15. IF SOMEONE COMES TO US FOR FORGIVNESS WE ARE TO FORGIVE THEM NO MATTER HOW DIFFICULT IT MAY BE.

16. WHETHER A DELIBERATE ACT OUR NOT WE MUST FOR GIVE.

17. FORGIVENESS BRINGS RELEIF.

1 Morally bad or wrong; wicked: an evil tyrant.

2 Causing ruin, injury, or pain; harmful: the evil effects of a poor diet.

3 Characterized by or indicating future misfortune; ominous: evil omens.

4 Bad or blameworthy by report; infamous: an evil reputation.

5 Characterized by anger or spite; malicious: an evil temper.

CHAPTER 13

EVIL

1. AND EVIL PERSON EXPOSES AND ONLY LOOKS FOR EVIL.

2. TEARING DOWN ONE FELLOW DOESN'T BUILD YOU UP ANY AT ALL.

3. WE ARE IN THIS TOGETHER DESTROYING ME ONLY DESTROYS YOU.

4. PLANNING MY FALL ONLY LEADS TO YOURS.

5. YOU PUT OUT TWENTY TIME THE EVIL PLOT FOR ME BUT YOU GOT TEN THOUSAND IN RETURN.

6. EVIL IN ANYWAY OR FORM IS WRONG.

7. THE LIAR ALWAYS COME WITH A POSSIE TO PROVE THERE CASE.

8. EVIL HAVE A WAY OF LOOKING SO PRETTY BUT UNDER ALL OF THAT IS DESTRUCTION.

9. EVIL DOERS WILL GET BY BUT THEY WONT GET AWAY.

10. AND EVIL PERSON WILL NEVER KNOW PEACE.

11. YOU CAN LET YOUR ATTITUDE GET YOU IN TROUBLE AND LATER HAVE REGRETS AND THEN YOU BECOME THE VICTIM.

12. A LIE TRYS TO HAVE LONGEVITY, BUT IT DOSENT HAVE ENOUGH STRENGTH TO LIVE.

13. WHEN YOU DO SOMETHING AND CAUSE TROUBLE DON'T BLAME ANYONE BUT YOURSELF.

14. DONT LET EVIL TAKE RESIDENT WITH YOU IT MAY SEEM GOOD FOR THE MOMENT BUT THE AFTER EFFECT WILL BRING SHAME.

15. WRONG IS NOTING TAUGHT WE ARE BORN WITH THAT RIGHT IS THE THING WE MUST BE TAUGHT.

16. IF YOU LOOK FOR FAULT YOU WILL FIND IT.IF YOU LOOK FOR GOOD YOU WILL FIND IT.

17. DOING THINGS OUT OF SPITE BRINGS TROUBLE TO US.

18. BEING A HATEFUL PERSON IS THE WORST THING WE CAN BE. REMEMBER TODAY FOR YOU TOMORROW FOR ME.

19. CHEATING SOMEONE OUT OF THERE INHERITANCE WILL LEAD YOU TO POVERTY.

20. WE CAN SEE THE FAULTS OF OTHERS BUT CAN'T SEE OURS.

21. DON'T REJOICE IN SOMEONE ELSES FAILURE.

22. DON'T GET HUNG UP IN DECEIT IT WILL NEVER WORK IN YOUR BEHALF.

23. SOME PEOPLE SAY THINGS TO MAKE YOU FEEL GOOD BUT WITH NO GOOD INTENTIONS.

24. JUST BECAUSE PEOPLE SMILE IN YOU FACE DON'T MAKE THEM YOUR FRIEND.

25. THE EVIL HOLD COVERSATIONS ABOUT THE JUST.

26. ONE THIEF DO TRUST THE OTHER.

27. DOING WRONG IN PRIVATE WILL SOONER OR LATER COME OUT IN THE OPEN.

28. EVIL CAN FALL UPON A GOOD PERSON JUST AS IT CAN AND EVIL.

Experience as a general concept comprises knowledge of or skill in or observation of some thing or some event gained through involvement in or exposure to that thing or event.

CHAPTER 14

EXPERIENCE

1. LOOKING AT THINGS WITH THE EYES MAKES IT LOOK EASY, UNTIL THE HANDS TRIES TO DO IT.

2. A NEW BROOM SWEEP CLEAN.

3. AND OLD CAPTAIN OF THE SHIP KNOWS THE CHANNELS.

4. THE THINGS WE LEARN IN LIFE ARE THE THINGS WE CHERISH THE MOST.

5. A GOOD COOK CAN PREPARE A GOOD MEAL WITHOUT HARDLEY TASTING IT.

6. ANY OLD FOOL CAN TEAR DOWN BUT IT TAKES A MAN OR WOMAN WITH EXPERIENCE TO BUILD.

7. KEEP ON LIVING YOU WILL UNDERSTAND LATER.

8. THERE ARE SOMETHINGS IN LIFE YOU JUST CAN'T IMAGINE YOU HAVE TO GO THROUGH IT TO UNDERSTAND.

9. THE MOST DIFFICULT THINGS IN LIFE CAN BECOME QUITE SIMPLE WITH TIME YOU CAN'T BEAT A PERSON WITH EXPERIENCE.

10. WHEN EVERYTHING IS STILL AND QUIET AND GOING WELL GET READY.

11. THE AGED MAN MUST BE THERE FOR THE YOUNG MAN JUST AS THE AGED WOMAN IS THERE FOR THE YOUNG WOMAN.

12. SLOW DOWN DON'T BE AS THE OLD BEAR MAKING A LOT OF TRACKS AND GETTING NO WHERE.

13. IT DOESN'T MATTER WHETHER YOU ARE RICH OR POOR EVERYONE HAVE A BIT OF KNOWLEDGE TO PASS ON FROM LIFE EXPERIENCES.

14. WE START OFF ONE WAY IN LIFE BUT EXPERIENCE HELPS US TO DO IT DIFFERENT.

15. THE HORN MAY BE THE LONGEST. BUT THE EARS ARE THE OLDEST.

16. BORROWING SOMETHING OLD CAN LEAD TO BUYING SOMETHING NEW.

17. I DON'T NEED A BOOK WHEN I SPEAK; I AM AT AN AGE NOW TO SPEAK FROM EXPERIENCE.

18. KNOWING IS NOT ENOUGH YOU NEED TO USE YOUR KNOW HOW.

19. A HEAP SEE BUT ONLY A FEW KNOW.

20. A PERSON LEARNS SOMETHING NEW NEARLY EVERYDAY. WHEN YOU STOP LEARNING IT USUALLY MEANS THAT YOU ARE DEAD.

21. EXPERIENCE TEACHES US CONTROL.

22. I CANT GIVE YOU EVERYTHING THERE ARE MANY THINGS YOU MUST LEARN ON YOUR OWN.

23. THINGS MAY BE DIFFERENT BUT WE ARE ALL STILL TRAVELING THE SAME ROAD.

24. A YOUNG MAN OR WOMAN MAKES MISTAKES AND OLDER MAN OR WOMAN WON'T.

25. EXPERIENCE SETTLES YOU.

26. THE NEARER THE SHORE THE HARDER THE BLOW.

27. EXPERIENCE TEACHES US HOW TO ADJUST.

28. WITHOUT GOING THROUGH THINGS IN THIS LIFE WE MAY FIND IT HARD TO UNDERSTAND HOW THINGS REALY ARE.

29. TO PROTECT YOURSELF WRITE IT DOWN.

30. THE WORST LOOKING FOOD TASTE THE BEST SOMETIME.

31. EXPERIENCE TEACHES YOU TO WAIT.

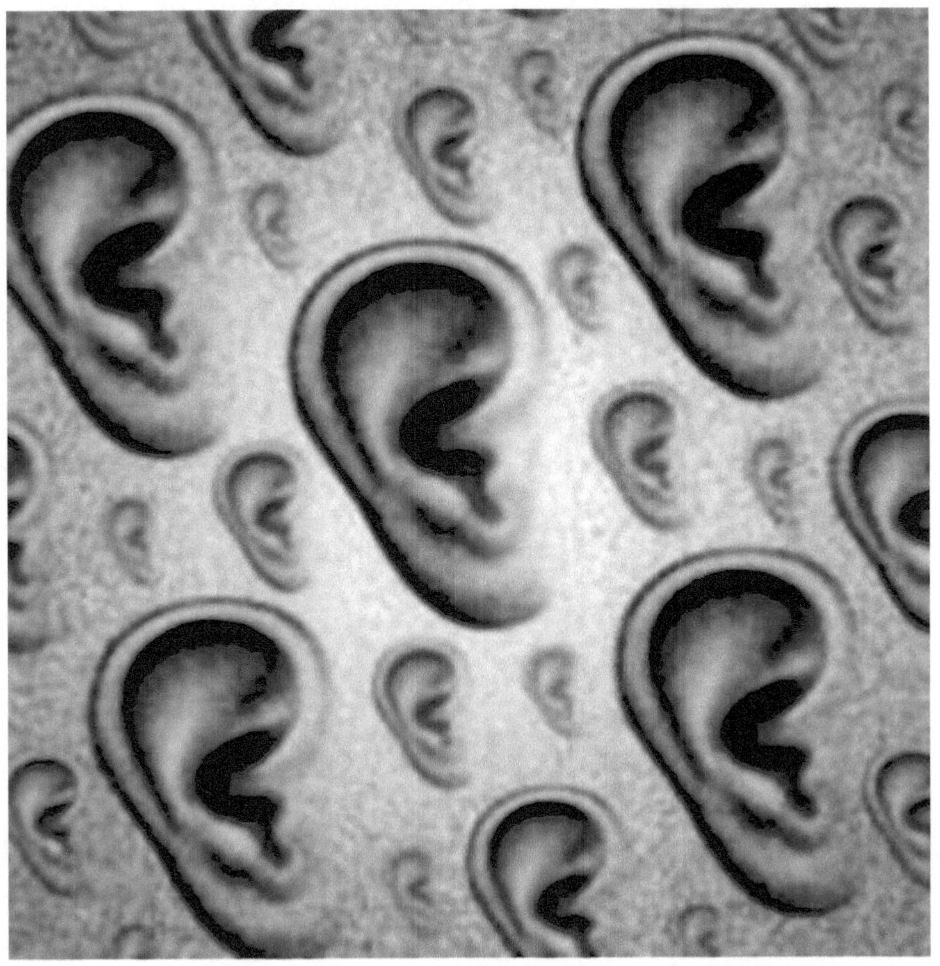

1: to pay attention to sound <listen to music>

2: to hear something with thoughtful attention : give consideration

CHAPTER 15

LISTEN

1. WE OFTEN LISTEN WITH OUR EARS BUT THERE COME TIME AND TIME AGAIN WE NEED TO LISTEN TO OUR HEART.

2. DADDY ALWAYS SAID ARE YOU LISTENING?

3. IF YOU ARE NOT SURE OF WHAT YOU HEARD ASK AGAIN.

4. IF YOU WANT A TRUE AND RIGHT ANSWER FIND A QUIET PLACE SIT STILL AND SILENT, PRAY, MEDITATE AND LISTEN.

5. IF YOU ARE BUSY LOOKING FOR ANSWERS JUST STOP LOOKING AND LISTEN.

6. THE GREATES ANSWER COMES WHEN WE BE STILL AND LISTEN.

1: to form or have in the mind

2: to have as an intention <thought to return early>

3: a : to have as an opinion <think it's so> b : to regard as : consider <think the rule unfair>

4: a : to reflect on : ponder <think the matter over> b : to determine by reflecting <think what to do next>

5: to call to mind : remember <he never thinks to ask how we do>

CHAPTER 16

THINK

1. AS AND ADULT DON'T BE CHILDISH IN YOUR THINKING.

2. DON'T EVER THINK IN THE NEGATIVE BE POSITIVE THINKING.

3. DON'T HANG AROUND WEAK MINDED PEOPLE. JUST BECAUSE YOU MAY NOT HAVE IT ALREADY DOESN'T MEAN THAT YOU WONT HAVE IT.

4. BE A THINKER. PEOPLE OF GREAT MINDS SEEK SOLUTIONS NOT EXCUSES.

5. A PERSON THAT THINKS DEEPLY COMES UP WITH ANSWERS THAT OTHERS MISS.

6. WHEN THERE IS NO ANSWER SOMEONE THAT IS A POWERFUL THINKER WILL FIND THE ANSWER.

7. IT ALWAYS PAYS TO THINK THINGS THROUGH OVER AND OVER AND OVER AND OVER AND OVER AGAIN.

8. SOMETHINGS WE CAN GIVE AND ANSWER QUICKLY, BUT THERE ARE THOSE TIMES WHEN QUICK WON'T DO.

9. WHEN EVER SOMEONE ASK FOR A RIGHT NOW OR QUICK ANSWER WATCH IT.

10. MAMA HAD A SAYING "DON'T USE YOUR HEAD FOR A HAT RACK THINK".

11. WE SHOULD NEVER TAKE ANYTHING FOR GRANTED NO MATTER HOW TEMPTING IT MAY BE.

12. DO YOU EVER TAKE TIME TO QUESTION YOURSELF WITH WHAT I AM ABOUT TO SAY OR DO IS IT GOING TO BE EFFECTIVE IN THE RIGHT WAY.

13. IF YOU DON'T THINK SOBERLY YOU NOT ONLY HURT YOURSELF LATER BUT ALL THAT ARE A PART OF YOU ALSO.

14. SOMEONE ELSE FALL IN LIFE DOESN'T LEAD TO YOUR FALL. YOU ONLY LEAD TO YOUR FALL.

15. IF I ONLY LOOK AT OTHERS THAT DO WRONG TO PACIFY MY WRONG, I AM A FOLLOWER OF WRONG AND BLIND TO DOING THE THINGS OF RIGHT.

16. A THINKER LEADS AND NOT NECCESARY AT THE FOREFRONT.

17. A PERSON MAY HAVE ABUNDANCE AND STILL BE A SMALL MINDED THINKER.

18. CREATING YOUR OWN HAPPINESS BY ANY MEANS CAN BE DEADLY.

19. HAVEING SOMETHING GOOD AND LETTING IT GO BECAUSE YOU THINK YOU FOUND SOMETHING BETTER IS FOOLISH YOU KNOW WHAT YOU HAVE. BUT YOU DON'T KNOW WHAT YOU ARE ABOUT TO GET. VISITING SOMEONE IS NOT THE SAME AS STAYING WITH THEM.

20. THERE ARE THOSE WHO FEEL I WORKED HARD TO GET HERE AND SO SHOULD EVERYONE ELSE. EACH ONE OF US HAVE A LEVEL OF INTELECT AND THERE ARE THOSE THAT WILL NEVER GET ANY HIGHER THAN THE MINIMIUM SOME AVERAGE, AND THEY SHOULDN'T BE PUNISHED BECAUSE THAT IS ALL THEY CAN DO.

21. IF YOU THINK ABOUT IT SOBERLY BEFORE HAND MOST LIKELY YOU WANT DO IT.

22. WE SHOULD LEARN TO LET GOOD ONLY BE IN OUR THOUGHTS.

WE ALL HAVE A CHOICE

CHAPTER 17
CHOICE

1. IF CHOICES IN LIFE ONLY AFFECT US THEN MAYBE IT WOULDN'T MATTER BUT SINCE IT AFFECTS EVERYONE AROUND US CHOOSE CAREFULLY.

2. IF YOU CHOOSE TO DO WRONG AND IT COMES BACK TO BITE YOU DON'T BLAME ANYONE BUT YOURSELF.

3. WHAT PEOPLE MAY THINK I DO DOSEN'T MATTER UNTIL THEY DO IT? AND LATER BE FULL OF REGRETS.

4. DON'T LET LUST ERODE YOUR THOUGHT PATTERN IT WILL ERODE YOU ALL TOGETHER.

5. IF SOMEONE MADE A BAD CHOICE AND LEARNED FROM IT AND TRY TO KEEP YOU FROM MAKING THE SAME MISTAKE THE WISE WOULD LISTEN THE FOOL WOULD REJECT.

6. BAD CHOICES CAN LEAD TO A LONG PATH OF HEART ACHES.

7. CHOOSE YOUR FRIENDS CAREFULLY MANY WILL CALL THEM SELF YOUR FRIEND JUST TO GIVE YOU ADVICE TO BRING PAIN TO YOU. THEY ARE TIRED OF FEELING IT ALL BY THEMSELVES.

8. NEVER MAKE ANY DECISION WITHOUT PRAYER.

9. CHOOSE RIGHT OVER WRONG AT ALL TIMES AND YOU WILL NEVER HAVE TO WORRY ABOUT CORRECTIONS LATER.

10. WHEN YOU ASK FOR HELP WITH A DECISION AND YOU MAKE THE FINAL DECISION AND IT DOSEN'T WORKOUT, DON'T BLAME ANYONE BUT YOURSELF YOU MADE THE FINAL DECISION.

11. YOU CAN'T CHOOSE WHO YOU ARE OR WHAT FAMILY YOU CAME FROM BUT YOU CAN MAKE RIGHT CHOICES TO CHANGE A PREVERSE FAMILY.

12. THE DECISIONS YOU MAKE WILL AFFECT EVERY ASPECT OF YOUR LIFE.

13. WHEN I WAS A CHILD MY PARENTS MADE CHOOSES FOR ME. NOW THAT I AM GROWN THE CHOICES ARE MINE.

14. EVERY CHOICE WE MAKE MAY NOT BE EXACTLY RIGHT BUT WE MUST CHOOSE.

15. SOME CHOICES WE MAKE ARE EASY SOME ARE NOT BUT THE DECISION IS OURS TO MAKE.

"So when they continued asking him, he lifted up himself, and said unto them, He that is without sin among you, let him first cast a stone at her." John 8:7

CHAPTER 18

JUDGEMENT

1. NEVER REACT WHEN YOU HAVE JUST ONLY CAUGHT THE BACK END OF THINGS.

2. WHEN OPPORTUNITY COMES KNOCKING AT OUR DOOR IT IS WISE TO TAKE ADVANTAGE OF IT. IT TAKES A VERY LONG TIME TO COME AROUND AGAIN.

3. ALL IT TAKES IS ONE EVENT IN A MAN LIFE TO CHANGE HIM FOR THE BETTER OR FOR THE WORST.

4. TO DO WRONG IS NEVER THE RIGHT THING TO DO.WRONG DOING ALWAYS HAVE ITS CONSEQUENCES TO DO WRONG TO SOMEONE THAT HAS DONE WRONG TO YOU WILL BRING MUCH WORSE RESULTS TO YOU IN THE END.

5. USE WISDOM NOT IMPULSE TO SETTLE MATTERS.

6. USE SOUND JUDGEMENT AND THINK THINGS THROUGH AND THROUGH AGAIN AND AFTER THAT DO IT AGAIN.

CHAPTER 19
CORRECTION

1. IF PEOPLE LOSE FAITH IN YOU. IT MAY BE HARD FOR THEM TO DEAL WITH YOU BUT WITH TIME AND PATIENCE THINGS CAN BE RESTORED. JUST DO THE RIGHT THING.

2. PAMPERING IS ALRIGHT IN ITS PLACE BUT THE BITTER MEDICINE IS THE ONE THAT DO US GOOD.

3. WHY DO WE STAND AROUND LOOKING AT THE DAMAGE THAT HAVE BEEN DONE LET US PICK UP THE PIECES AND BUILD AGAIN.

4. A LAZY CHILD CAN CAUSE PROBLEMS IN THE HOME.

5. PUT THE RUBBING WHERE THE PAIN IS.

6. TIME OF CORRECTION CAN BE VERY HARD.

7. CORRECTION DOESN'T USUALLY COME WITHOUT PAIN.

1. Mental power, force, or vigor.
2. Moral power, firmness, or courage.
3. Power by reason of influence, authority, resources, numbers, etc.

CHAPTER 20

STRENGTH

1. FELLING SORRY FOR OURSELVES HAVING A PITTY PARTY DOESN'T AMOUNT TO BUT SO MUCH AND NO MORE. GOING DOWN IS ONE THING WHAT YOU DO WHEN YOU GET UP IS ANOTHER. EVEN A BABY WHEN THEY ARE IN THE PROCESS OF LEARNING TO WALK. WHEN THEY FALL THEY KNOW TO GET UP AND NO MATTER HOW MANY TIMES THEY FALL THEY JUST KEEP GETTING UP. IF THEY FALL AND IT HURT THEY LEARN TO PROCEED WITH CAUTION YOU WOULD SEE THEM GRAB HOLD TO THE TABLE OR CHAIR OR SOMEONE OR SOMETHING TO HELP GET THERE BALANCE. SO MUST WE KEEP TRYING WHETHER IT LEAD TO SOMETHING SMALL OR SOMETHING GREAT BUT TO WHAT EVER IT AMOUNT TO JUST KEEP GETTING UP.

2. THE TEMPLE YOU CARRY AROUND WITH YOU EVERYDAY SOMETIMES CAN COME UNDER ATTACK FOR NO REASON. BUT WITH THIS TEMPLE YOU CAN OVER COME ANYTHING.

3. YOU MAY NEVER KNOW WHAT KIND OF STRENGTH YOU HAVE UNTIL YOU ARE TRIED.

4. TOGETHER STRENGTH YOU MUST GO THROUGH PAIN.

5. THE STRONG WILL ENDURE PAIN TO BECOME A VICTOR.

6. YOU MUST GO THROUGH A PROCESS TO BECOME STRONG.

7. STRENGTH IS ON A PATHWAY THAT COME WITH MORE DIFFICULTY THAN MANY WILL WANT TO ENDURE.

1. a false statement made with deliberate intent to deceive; an intentional untruth; a falsehood.

CHAPTER 21

LIES

1. A LIE MAY TRY TO LIVE FOREVER BUT IT DOESN'T HAVE THE STERNGTH TO.

2. YOU SET YOUR OWNSELF UP WHEN YOU LIE TO ANYONE.

3. A LIE MAY SEEM EASY AT THE TIME BUT IT WILL COME BACK.

4. LIES RUN TRUTH STAND STILL AND WHEN LIES GET THROUGH RUNNING IT RUNS BACK INTO TRUTH.

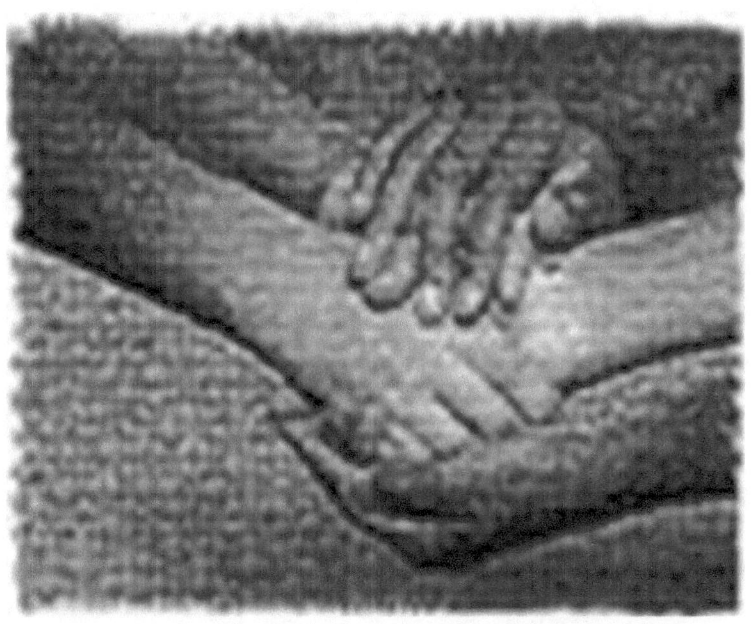

PROVERBS 12:26 26 The righteous is more excellent than his neighbour: but the way of the wicked seduceth them.

CHAPTER 22

FRIEND

1. TO FIND A TRUE FRIEND IS TO FIND A JEWEL.

2. WE MUST EMBRACE PEACE AS A DEAR FRIEND.

3. A FRIEND WILL BE ONE OF YOUR GREATEST SUPPORTERS.

4. YOU CAN PUT TRUST IN A FRIEND.

5. A FRIENDS LOVE NEVER RUNS OUT.

"Weeping may endure for a night, but joy cometh in the morning"
Psalms 30:5

CHAPTER 23

JOY

1. GOOD NEWS MAKES THE HEART HAPPY.

2. PEACE AND HAPPINESS IN A HOME KEEPS IT TOGETHER.

3. TEARS OF JOY COME FROM A HAPPY HEART.

4. KEEPING THE HEART HAPPY PROLONG LIFE.

5. MONEY CAN TURN A FROWN INTO A SMILE.

6. HAPPINES IN THE HEART CAN BRING JOY UNKNOWN.

Proverbs 19:22—What is desirable in a person is kindness, and it is better to be poor than a liar.

CHAPTER 24

KINDNESS

1. ANY AMOUNT OF KINDNESS CAN DO SO MUCH GOOD.

2. A HUG CAN MEAN SO MUCH.

3. A KIND WORD CAN MAKE SOMEONE DAY GO A LOT BETTER.

4. WE MUST LEARN TO BE CONSIDERATE TO EACH OTHER.

mental process of a person who comprehends; comprehension; personal interpretation

CHAPTER 25

UNDERSTANDING

1. HAVING AND UNDERSTANDING BETWEEN EACH OTHER CAN SAVE A WORLD OF PAIN.

2. TALKING THING THROUGH ALWAYS WORKS BETTER THAN ARGUING THINGS THROUGH.

3. ASKING AGAIN CAN STOP PROBLEMS AND GIVE A CLEAR UNDERSTANDING.

4. IF WE THINK WE ARE GOING TO BE HAPPY ALL THE TIME WE MAY BE FOOLING OURSELVES, WITH ALL THE GOOD DAYS WE ALSO WILL HAVE THE BAD.

5. JUST BECAUSE SOMETHING HAVEN'T HAPPEN TO US YET. DOSEN'T MEAN IT WANT HAPPEN TO US IN TIME.

6. WE CAN OFTIME MAKE GREAT DECISIONS AND SPEAK BOLDLY AND SAY WHAT WE WANT DO WHILE THINGS ARE IN OUR FAVOR.ONLY PEOPLE OF UNDERSTANDING DEAL THROUGH THINGS WITH TIME AND PATIENCE NOT ON INSTINCT.

7. DON'T LET BAD EXPERIENCES CAUSE YOU TO BECOME A BAD PERSON.

8. DON'T DO ANYTHING FOR A DOLLAR THERE MAY COME A TIME THAT YOU MAY NOT GET TO SPEND IT.

9. DON'T LET THE PRESSURE OF YOUR DAY RUIN THE DAY FOR OTHERS.

10. GETTING INVOLVE WITH YOUR CHILDREN KEEPS THEM FROM GETTING INVOLVED WITH TROUBLE.

11. IF WE DON'T TEACH OUR CHILDREN TO STAND UP FOR THEM SELVES THEY MAY ENTER INTO A LIFE OF VIOLENCE BECAUSE OF FEAR.

12. NOT DOING SOMETHING FOR OTHERS BECAUSE YOU THINK IT WANT EFFECT YOU IS SUCH A MISCONCEPTION WHAT EFFECT ONE WILL SOONER OR LATER AFFECT THE OTHER.

13. LOVE IN THE HOME IS SOMETHING THAT SHOULD NEVER BE LEFT OUT NO MATTER HOW BUSY OR HOW TIRED WE MAY BE KEEP LOVE ABOARD.

14. IF YOU DON'T LIKE SOMEONE JUST LEAVE THEM ALONG. DON'T TRY TO DESTROY THEM BECAUSE OF YOUR FEELING. TIME BRING ON CHANGES WHAT YOU DO TO THEM WILL COME BACK TO YOU MUCH WORSE.

15. WE MUST DO THE THINGS TO DEVELOP A STRONG MIND AND BODY. TO PREVENT THE SUFFERING OF EITHER ONE.

16. SPORTY CARS AND FANCY HOMES DOSEN'T ALWAYS MEAN PLENTY OF MONEY.

17. WHEN A PERSON FIND THEMSELVES FUSSING WITHOUT A RESPONSE THEY WILL STOP.

18. WE START LIFE ALONG AND WE WILL END IT ALONG.

19. LET US SPEND MORE TIME UNDERSTANDING EACH OTHER.

20. DO NOT GO BEYOND WHAT YOU ABLE TO DO JUST TO IMPRESS OTHERS IT CAN BRING YOUR FALL.

21. STRENGTH IS SOMETHING WE ALL SHOULD POSSESS IN OUR LIFE BUT DON'T THINK BECAUSE YOU ARE STRONG THAT YOU CANT FALL.

22. A QUIET PERSON LISTENS A BLABBER MOUTH TELLS EVERYTHING.

23. A SMALL CHILD CAN TOUCH A WOMAN BODY AND GET AWAY WITH IT BUT A GROWN UP CANNOT DO THE SAME.

24. DON'T TAKE A PERSON OUT TO EAT WHEN THEY SAY THEY ARE NOT HUNGRY.

25. LITTLE PEOPLE CAN EAT A LOT.

26. WE MUST MAKE A MARK IN LIFE FOR OURSELF.

27. YOU DON'T KNOW WHAT THE OTHER PERSON IS GOING THROUGH AND BEING RUDE TO THEM WON,T HELP.

28. TREAT PEOPLE WITH RESPECT AND IT WILL COME BACK TO YOU.

29. WE ALL HAVE TALENT AND SKILLS SEEK OUT THE BEST ONES FOR YOU AND GO FOR IT.

30. ALWAYS DEAL WITH UNDERSTANDING.

31. IN ORDER TO HAVE PERFECT HARMONY WE MUST HAVE THE POOR MIDDLE CLASS AND THE RICH FOR WITHOUT IT WE ALL SUFFER.

32. DON'T LET YOURSELF GET HUNG UP ON WHAT YOU ARE GOING THROUGH IN THIS LIFE ALWAYS LOOK AT WERE YOU ARE HEADED TO AND YOU WILL ENCOURAGE YOURSELF.

33. NO MATTER HOW GOOD YOU ARE TO MANY SOME WILL STILL TURN AROUND AND HURT YOU.

34. A ZEBRA MAY NOT BE ABLE TO CHANGE ITS STRIPS BUT A PERSON CAN CHANGE THERE WAYS.

35. WE OFTEN TIMES COME ACROSS PEOPLE WHO HAVE THIS WAY OF THINKING IT CAN'T HAPPEN TO ME AS

LONG AS YOU ARE ALIVE YOU STAND THE CHANCE OF IT HAPPENING.

36. YOU CAN ALWAYS COME HOME AFTER LIFE SURPRISE.

37. ONLY A FOOLISH PERSON WON'T RECEIVE CORRECTION.

38. YOU SHOULD NEVER REST AT THE SURFACE OF ANYTHING BUT GO DOWN TO THE ROOT.

39. THE SUN LIGHT IS SO IMPORTANT TO OUR HEALTH. BUT TO STARE DIRECTLY INTO IT CAN TAKE OUR EYE SIGHT AWAY.

40. IF WE CAN ALL COME TO THE UNDERSTANDING THAT EACH CULTURE IS DIFFERENT AND TAKE THE TIME TO UNDERSTAND EACH OTHER WE WOULD ALL BE BETTER OFF.

41. EACH WOMAN MAY HAVE THE SAME AND SO DOES EACH MAN BUT YET THERE ARE DIFFRENCES.

42. NO MATTER HOW LONG IT TAKES YOU WILL SOON OR LATER GET TIRED.

43. SUMMER TIME WE LOOK FOR THE SHADE WINTER TIME WE LOOK FOR THE SUN.

44. TAKE WHAT YOU HAVE AND MAKE WHAT YOU WANT.

45. DONT THINK BECAUSE YOU HAVE BEEN DOWN SO MANY TIMES THAT YOU WONT GET UP BECAUSE EVERTIME YOU GET UP STRENGTH COMES UP WITH YOU.

46. WHEN YOU GO THROUGH A TRANSFORMATION YOU MY NOT BE UNDERSTOOD DON'T LET IT DISCOURAGE YOU.

47. YOU CAN NOT DO IT ALL ON YOUR OWN YOU WILL NEED HELP.

48. LEARN TO FOLLOW BEFORE YOU WORRY ABOUT LEADING.

49. EVERYONE WANTS TO LEAD BUT EVERYONE IS NOT A LEADER.

50. YOU CANNOT CARRY EVERYONE BURDENS YOU HAVE ALL YOU NEED CARRING YOUR OWN.

51. REACH THE SPIRIT OF THE MAN AND YOU REACH THE MAN.

52. WE WERE ALL MADE AND ORIGINAL BUT SOME OF US JUST ONLY KNOW HOW TO BE A COPY.

53. WHEN WE WERE YOUNG FOR SOME REASON OUR A ANOTHER WE WANTED TO BE A GROWN UP AND WHEN WE GET OLD MANY TIMES WE WANT TO GO TO THE BACK OF THE LINE.

54. DON'T RUSH A CHILD INTO ADULT HOOD THEY WILL HAVE PLENTY OF TIME TO BE AND ADULT.

55. A FEW MOMENT OF PLEASURE NOW CAN CAUSE A LOT OF PAIN LATER.

56. I INTEND ON LIVING A LONG LIFE BUT IF YOU HERE THAT I AM GONE ON TOMORROW JUST REMEMBER I COULDN'T HELP IT.

57. A POOR MAN MAKE ARRANGEMENT A RICH MAN DO BUSINESS.

58. EVEN THOUGH YOU MAY UNDERSTAND THE WAY OF LIFE AFTER TIME AND AGE YOU STILL KNOW NOT TO TAKE SHORT CUTS.

59. SHORT CUTS CAN MAKE A TRIP A JOURNEY.

60. EVERYTHING GOES THROUGH A PROCESS.

61. BEING YOUNG PARENTS WE DON'T UNDERSTAND WHY OUR PARENTS AS GRANDPARENTS SEEM TO CHANGE INTO THIS PERSON. THAT WOULD PUT IT TO US. BUT WHEN GRAND KIDS COME ALONG THEY ARE SO LOVEY DOVEY THEY ARE SO GLAD TO SEE THE GRANDS AND GIVE SO MUCH LOVE AND AFTER A FEW DAYS OF THE GRANDS BEING AROUND PLAYING THEY ARE READY TO SEND THEM BACK HOME MAYBE THEY HAVE CHANGED THAT MUCH.

62. A GOOD HUSBAND OR WIFE WOULD UNDERSTAND THAT THEY ARE THE BEST THING THEY HAVE GOING FOR THEMSELVES OTHER THAN GOD.

63. WHEN A PARENT DO THE JOB RIGHT AS A PARENT MANY TIME THE CHILD WOULD THINK OF WAYS TO RUN AWAY FROM HOME.

64. EVEN CHILDREN DONT LIKE TO FOLLOW ORDERS MANY TIME THEY MAY GET UPSET BUT THEY MUST DO.MANY ADULTS HAVE THE SAME TENDENCY AND KEEP CAUSING PROBLEMS IN THERE LIVES.

65. CHILDREN ARE TO BE TAUGHT.

66. DO THE RIGHT THING AND YOUR CHILDREN WILL GIVE YOU THE HONOR.

67. CHILDREN HAVE AWAY OF TRYING TO MAKE YOU FEEL SORRY FOR THEM IN THERE WRONG BE THE ADULT, AND DO THE RIGHT THING.

68. FOR A PARENT TO HUG THERE CHILD GIVES THEM A FEELING THAT NOTHING ELSE CAN DESCRIBE.

69. GIVING A CHILD EVERYTHING ISNT THE SAME AS RAISING THEM.

70. FINDING TIME TO RAISE SOMEONE ELSES CHILD AND NOT TAKE TIME TO RAISE YOUR OWN CAN COME WITH BACK LASHES.

71. THERE IS NEVER A CONVENIENT TIME TO RAISE CHILDREN YOU JUST DO YOUR BEST.

72. EVERY PARENT WHO HAVE RAISED THERE CHILDREN HAVE HAD SOME TYPE OF STRUGGLE ONE WAY OR ANOTHER.

73. HAVING A CHILD CAN COME WITH SO MUCH JOY BUT IT CAN ALSO COME WITH STRUGGLE BUT FIGHT IT OUT THEY WILL GROW UP.

74. EVERY GOOD THING COMES FROM GOD OUR CHILDREN ARE A BLESSING FROM GOD SO THEY ARE GOOD.

www.ingramcontent.com/pod-product-compliance
Lightning Source LLC
Chambersburg PA
CBHW031249280526
45784CB00004B/1777

* 9 7 8 1 4 6 5 3 0 7 5 8 3 *